SUTTON SONNETS

A Celebration of Civic Pride

Immanuel Gaskin

AN

i AM
SM1

BOOK

Published by **iAM SM1**

www.imagconsciousdesign.com/i-am-sm1/

First Published 2024

Printed by Kindle Direct Publishing

ISBN

978-1-7394915-3-6

Contents

Introduction

This book starts with a sonnet, a parody of a Shakespearean sonnet, that is describing the local High Street:

Sutton '22: Shall I compare you to the Purley Way?

Shall I compare you to the Purley Way?

Thou art more street like but more desperate:

Tough times do shape your terrace shop displays,

And expensive leases making emptiness, to date

Sometimes I see the retail lines

More prominent as the black barber trimmed

Sign of times or time of signs

Opposite glimmers the full capacity gym

But the unbearable hot summer cannot rest on a fade!

The high street must adapt for growth

But new migrants bring new awning and shade

Heralds diversity and prosperity both

So as long as the merchants cross the sea

They will be serving the local customers, so also me.

Parody of "Sonnet 18: Shall I compare thee to a summer's day?" by William Shakespeare

This poem was made for my first poetry book SUBSTITUTIONS. It challenged me to think of interesting ways to parody great works of poetry by the greatest of poets.

The main thing about conducting the parody exercise with this sonnet was, it caused me to reflect on the nature of my hometown and then ponder its failures, successes and its future.

The next poem was written for a local competition for a Remembrance Garden in response to the Covid pandemic that swept the world. Many people were lost to illness brought on by symptoms of the pandemic. The winning poems were to be placed on a lectern near the main local hospital. My poem did not get selected for this, but was commended by the judges, and was later published in a local council community newsletter.

The poem gave me time to ponder on the wonderful architecture of St Helier hospital where I was born and the, then recent, passing away and the strangely poetic connection between my Godmother Carol and best friend Nic through the word "Aultone". A word at once being both a road name and a band name. It was also a meditation on the wit and humour displayed in conversations during local walks I would take with my young son. I would look across at the splendid vistas, that would opportunely present themselves, afforded to us by the many vantage points on hills throughout the borough. I would point out a shimmering almost ethereal white building on the horizon, where I first met the world, and then would weave a tale:

Remember There is a Palace on the Hill

I joked to my son that I was born in a white shining palace on a hill!
As we take vantage point across the borough, you see it still.

It glistens
And it listens
To each beating heart!

It has tales of the nation's heroes,
And of each family's heroes
As on their next journey
They have had to depart!

I said goodbye to a Godmother and best friend,
Joined by Aultone Ways

I found it hard to comprehend.
But both had their ways, to tell you their truth.
I ponder them both in age and youth.

So I am thanking them both
For loving and sharing.

The same to St Helier, my white palace of caring.

I thank the staff, all knights for
Effortlessly giving,

And I thank you in this garden
For reflecting and remembering.
So please, please, Please!
Celebrate them and yourselves through living.

You can find both poems in my books SUSTITUTIONS and NO SUSTITUTIONS.

These two poems in isolation where great opportunities to think about my home borough, the London Borough of Sutton, through a more thoughtful filter. It made me question could it be better? It made me wonder how do I make more connections, in the area where I lost the presence of two strong foundations that were my family and my friend?

In the journey of searching for the answers it became clear that the community may have similar questions and journeys. They may find themselves sometimes spotting the negative things locally and neglecting to convey the positives and show their love.

So I created a brand iAM SM1 and part of it ethos was to talk up the town and bring us together. The first idea was to identify iconic buildings and areas in the town centre of Sutton, in London (For those who may argue that it is not!!!). Then record it with photos and then use my sketching over and architectural training and presentation skills to make images of these icons.

Sutton Library was the starting point. It was something to be proud of. A world leading library and a civic campus and citadel holding an adult education college and council offices and chambers. The place taught us how to read and make clay pots, kept people warm when politics left them cold and personally helped me find my first job in an architectural office. The place was laudable and so very iconic it had to be celebrated and commemorated.

And the same could be said for other parts of the borough.

When all of the above thoughts and themes came together momentum and magic manifested itself.

Each of the poems and the first Sutton Icon image inspired more of each.

This book shares 12 new sonnets and 12 drawings of local icons.

This is SUTTON SONNETS.

All the artwork and images were drawn, coloured in and made by Immanuel Gaskin.

List of works:

1. Sutton Library

2. Carshalton Theatre

3. Manor Park, Sutton

4. Sutton Cinema

5. The Cock Sutton

6. Sutton High St -Trinity Square

7. St Helier Hospital, Carshalton

8. Sutton Arena

9. Sutton Arcade

10. The Attic -St Nicholas Centre

11. Sutton Register Office – The Russettings

12. Hackbridge Community Garden

Dedicated to places and people that we all love

And call home.

Dedicated to everyone who supports

iAM SM1

Read it carefully:

I am someone

(Yes, you are!)

ONE

Sutton Library: Quilt

A bastion of civic hopes and pride,

Red bricks, rectilinear, still modern

Adult learning, books expertly set aside

For community, so never forgotten.

Seventies construction, holding dreams.

The Councillors like channelled beserkers

Minutes and discourse held in paper reams

Home to the diligent Council workers.

Learners of guitar or skilled pottery,

Adjacent to racks of literature.

Its cornucopia, the lottery!

Community serving its main feature.

Conglomeration of concept plus thoughts.

A wonderful playground of all its parts.

TWO

Cryer Arts : Who is Charles Cryer?

Why is a Cryer important to art?

Once public hall, theatre and roller rink

One of a company who played their part

Enclosing space for Carshalton to link.

Could have been closed, bar hope and a save

From lack of footfall or specialist know.

A Borough with no drama? You need brave!

When a building is empty there is no show!

Charles Cryer was a believer! So true.

Loved arts counsel and Carshalton pantos

Observant locals knew they had to do

Something engaging. Everyday heroes.

Though heroes of the past may not last long,

Herald new believers bringing new song!

Carshalton   Theatre

THREE

Manor Park

"Not on my Manor!" I heard you just say!

"Yes in my manner" sings the minstrel folk

Bigger parks in the borough to go play.

Everyone enters. No Manor house? The joke.

From war monument to lovely fountain,

Green Hedges, hay bale cafe to wood benches.

Kids have slides and their climbing frame mountains.

Adults have tea and cordial quenches.

Central and vital, it even has friends

Taking pride and time to nurture each day

That Mother nature generously sends

Each plant, grass blade,shower, and sun ray.

Off the High Street being still very stately

The community benefits greatly.

i AM
SM1

I Gaskin   Manor Park Sutton.

FOUR

Sutton Cinema

Numerically named "the Studio

One, two", three glamourous magical Screens.

Celluloid dreams of fairytales you know,

Or of action packed drama movie scenes.

Happy kids when the film's Universal

The romance with pictures, not static.

Date night couples seek controversial

A blockbuster, arthouse, noir or Classic

The last standing cinema of the area

After there was dancing, the tale? Complex!

A development spelling the end of era

To the St Nicholas Way multiplex.

As one cinema shuts,another opens

As the biggest dreamers exchange tokens

FIVE

The Cock Hotel

The Sutton population know their way

Deftly and willfully around The Cock!

Standing proud, erect, "Magnificent" they say.

It's a hotel sign near an office block.

Once the hostelry of a pugilist

Fighting bareback, bareknuckle!

A mislocated relic. Hard to miss.

No pub, no inn, not a saddle buckle

A sign without an obvious function.

No mythology of the champion.

A functioning signpost at a junction.

No monument to Gentleman Jackson.

Memorial? Folly? Anomaly?

Locals, laugh and snigger at what they see!

The Cock, Sutton

SIX

Trinity Square

Foolhardy making a Trinity Square!

What qualities could make a street so high?

The fact of existence show that they dare

Make crossroads, in the town, where you buy.

Be it hardware, be it coffee or books,

You get burgers and markets through seasons.

Christmas trees, protests and bystanders' looks.

You will get there for many of reasons.

Trees and greenery soften hard and stark,

While drinkers and thinkers find them a seat.

Benches, murals, an opticians, the park

Can be viewed from where vantage points meet.

The value of rounding up three to four

Is, community really gets much more.

Sutton High Street

I Cashin

SEVEN

St Helier Hospital

The exceptional care is so thorough

St Helier Hospital is just great!

Births and healing find place in the borough.

Both landmark and beacon on the Estate.

Nurses of Windrush, now the Philippines

And never forget the unsung local,

Extraordinary human beings!

For their endeavours we must be vocal!

Departments with poor funding or closure,

Accident and emergency at threat,

Let's not let austerity get closer

We each owe it an everlasting debt!

So campaign, debate and stay healthy, please.

The Saint needs us, now it is on its knees.

St Helier Hospital, Carshalton

I Goshan

EIGHT

Sutton Arena

Run, with bad stitch run, for goodness or fun

The olympiad gods will have seen ya

On Indoor and outdoor tracks, rain or sun

As you train there at Sutton Arena.

Borough champions born out of cinder!

Hopping, skipping, Jumping , higher, long

For the measuring tape is a winder

All of this effort will make you so strong.

From paralympian dedication

To legs, posterior and tums classes.

Community giving Inspiration.

Homemade energy fit for the masses.

Catering for the sporting elite call,

But resonates firmly as sport for all!

NINE

Sutton Arcade

My disappointment in Sutton Arcade,

Is that its glory is Arcadia,

But in truth no Arcade games played,

My nostalgia, which is crazier.

From park to High Street such longing

Past time rummaging for a comic book.

Off the main thoroughfare but belonging,

To an ambitious and grandiose look.

Another case for the Arcadian

Nostalgia talked about in a Half daze.

Fitting testament to Victorian

Ingenuity. Seventies half days!

In collective memories connection!

Its removal natural selection.

TEN

The Attic

Crowning Jewel of a centre of shopping.

Home of the baked, seasoned cuisine or fry.

When you have so little time for stopping

Just seek wonderment of a crystal sky

It brings forth so elegantly the World.

Korean and pizza, Caribbean lunches

Prepared fresh, hospitality unfurled

Such elegance witnessed between crunches.

But did you blink, in passing and miss it

Transcendent! Our glass roofed Eiffel Tower, that

Is so captivatingly explicit,

Whether escalating, standing or sat!

So lose it or go out and enjoy it!

It has food, a globe, glass and such spirit!

The Attic, Sutton

LEVEL 3   LEVEL 3

I AM SM1

I Gaskin

ELEVEN

The Russettings

A testament to birth, deaths and marriage

Important for them to administer

Horse drawn or modern motorised carriage.

Community names on the register

Sausages, ice creams and a wed sister,

Famous architect, husband, initials

Now home of the professional lister,

Registrar, nuptials & rituals.

Nestled discreetly in the quiet street,

Incognito presence you will find

From Thomas Wall to emulating Fleet,

Talking papers weekly to the blind.

A house? Home to multitudes of things.

This is the ballad of The Russettings.

Sutton Register Office, Russettings

I.Gashin

TWELVE

Hackbridge Community Garden

Like a shepherd, without a flock of sheep,

Enter Brazilian sculptural artist,

Seeks scrubland without an upkeep,

Then, makes a big difference regardless!

Creates a studio, a bivouac,

To make alchemy from what he can find.

Spotted what the area lacked,

His tender love with his actions, so kind.

But after such generosity he leaves!

Not a dry eye, the side stream gets wetter

Then the neighbourhood flock starts to believe:

"Continue like that driven Go-getter!"

Brings great pleasure, we see they work hard on,

Loving Hackbridge Community Garden

Hackbridge Community Garden

I Gaskin

Conclusion

And there concludes this part of my journey.

We have a book that has12 images that I feel are iconic to Sutton and 12 sonnets that begin to explore the history or the atmosphere and nostalgia of each place.

Looking at the icons linguistically, analytically and artistically and responding to them in sketches with a digital pen or on a keyboard through words, created a deeper understanding of each place and a stronger connection to them.

I have had great conversations with the community about buildings, parks and places that they love and why they love them.

I have had the opportunity to research and discover, architects, artist, benefactors, councillors and the community both from the past and present.

What has been so wonderful about creating this book is that the places and stories and people all come to life. It is almost as if you are in the same space even though most of the people and some of the place are long gone or are even scheduled to go.

This book has let me resurrect places that have been demolished and are just distant memories too.

However as you talk to the community and trawl through books and the internet they are still there. This is very reassuring in world dealing with change and a need for things to be fit for modern purpose.

I could give you all the stories now, but where is the fun in that.

This is your jumping off point.

Time to decide:

- Do you want to know more about the 1st twelve icons and seek them out?
- Or could your journey be to create your own poems, pictures and research?

My only advice is to think of a project that inspires you and pursue it.

The rewards will be even greater than the initial brief and task you set yourself.

This is what SUTTON SONNETS and iAM SM1 has done for me.

Author's Biography

Immanuel Gaskin is a British - born poet, an award-winning Architect and a community artist who had found a lifelong love of poetry starting at English lessons at school and has enjoyed the journey it has taken him on from adventures with film poets to the open mic and to collaborations with musicians as well as producing his own spoken word albums.

2012 - Releases 2 spoken word albums on Soundcloud as IMAG_Conscious Design entitled Hollingdeanland and Thistopian Community Picnic plus a bonus music album in the same year entitled Colander from a butter pan. All reflections on race across the generations, the malaise of being middle class and the beloved 90s music and TV and film scores of his youth.

2015 - Writer of the poem "Come Fall with me" adapted into a dance track "Fall with Me" by Sumsuch & Matty Eeles and released by Color & Pitch Records.

2021 – Whose Poem is it Anyway? – Creative Connections Festival – Invited Artist to give a community spoken word and poetry workshop in an online festival in conjunction with Arts Network Sutton and Department for Digital, Culture, Media & Sport and National Lottery Community Fund.

2021 - His poem "Remember there is a palace on the hill!" - Was a Commended Poem in the Sutton Poetry Project: Covid Remembrance & Reflection Poetry Competition run by the London Borough of Sutton Council.

2023 - He is always looking for ways to produce, learn, collaborate and inspire through the arts, creativity and mentoring. SUBSTITUTIONS is the first published entry into this ethos. This was followed by the short story poetry book CLOUD SOFA, an inspirational allegory based on a sofa discarded in the street. NO SUBSTITUTIONS a collection of the poetry of a lifetime brought together in print for the 1st time also published in a prolific year of production.

2024 – Sutton Icons Canvas, his images of local Iconic buildings places and spaces, exhibited in the historic Vellum Mill Gallery in Carshalton. SUTTON SONNETS is published with the Sutton Icon images with accompanying poetic verse.

About iAM SM1

I am publishing this short book under the "i AM SM1" Brand.

There are 3 things that i AM SM1 would like to do:

- Empower the local community with a slogan of pride for the area.
- Starting conversations about ideas and be a listening ear to local people and by doing so help to create a stronger community.
- Make and sell products with the slogan on to continue to show pride for the London Borough of Sutton and the Areas it contains.

This book is about building a community. We can all create and thrive. We can all make and sell. The local community reminded me that I was a poet and encouraged me to share my experience of making spoken word audio and the writing process of poems honed over the last 30 plus years.

I was keen to share and wanted my 1st published works to be a way to connect with and have a conversation with poets, who are and poets who are yet to be and needed a little mentoring push and the local community at large.

The objective to me was can I write a book? The answer is now yes there are 3 books before this to explore.

Can it inspire others to do it or at least inspire them to start writing a poem or connect with their community? You tell me!

Contact me at iamstillsm1@gmail.com to tell me your journey or about your poems, creative ventures or the book you are going to publish.

This is my 4th attempt at publishing an official book and yes I know it is intentionally short but, as always, It did take a lot of time and love to craft and I have some more in the pipeline. I hope once you start your journey you will say the same. Looking forward to seeing them.

If you got this far and are local (or a budding poet) here is a bonus sheet from the workshop. Finish off the last line in the grey spaces provided. Personalise your Sutton Sonnets book. The workshop inspired me. I hope the same is true for you!

Whose Poem is it Anyway?
Write your Lines in the Spaces

There is a Hadrian like wall,
By St Philomena's that leads
To Carshalton by the sea!

.....

There is a shard of glass
Heralding the yuletide arrival
Of Saint Nicholas

.....

When the snowfalls,
Or the environmental minstrels call,
And the Catherine wheel spins
In the dip

.....

We all love our borough
Hey, we care for each other
Because Sutton's
London's Jewel in the Crown.

.....

YOU (2021)

Printed in Great Britain
by Amazon